Alaskan
ICE CLIMBING

Rob Waring, *Series Editor*

HEINLE
CENGAGE Learning

Australia • Brazil • Japan • Korea • Mexico • Singapore • Spain • United Kingdom • United States

Words to Know

This story starts in Talkeetna [tælkiːtnə] in Alaska, in the United States (U.S.). It ends in an area called Matanuska [mætənuːskə], near Denali [dənɑːli] National Park.

A **In the Mountains.** Here are some activities you can do on a mountain or a glacier. Match the words in the box to the correct picture.

climbing	hiking	skiing

1. _____ 2. _____ 3. _____

The Matanuska **Glacier** is over 27 miles long.

B Mountain Weather Conditions. Weather refers to the conditions in the sky and air. Match each weather word to the correct definition.

1. cloud: _____

2. fine: _____

3. fog: _____

4. ice: _____

5. rain: _____

6. snow: _____

7. sunshine: _____

8. wind: _____

a. the light from the sun

b. very cold water that has become hard

c. a natural, fast movement of air

d. white frozen water that falls from the sky in cold weather

e. a white or grey mass in the air made from small drops of water

f. drops of water falling from the sky

g. good or nice

h. a heavy grey mass near the ground that makes it difficult to see

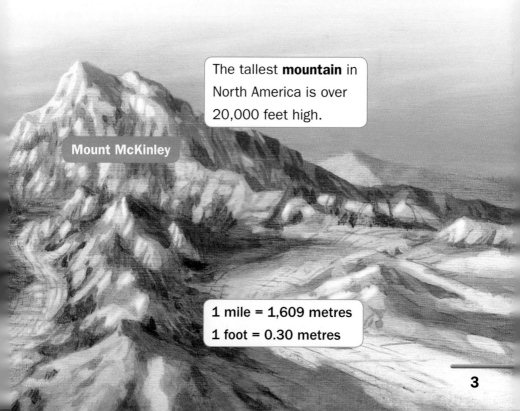

The tallest **mountain** in North America is over 20,000 feet high.

Mount McKinley

1 mile = 1,609 metres
1 foot = 0.30 metres

There's only one thing that's certain about the weather in Alaska—it changes all the time! Sometimes there's rain, sometimes there's wind and sometimes there's snow. Sometimes the weather is just fine with lots of sunshine.

On one particular day, there's rain and fog all the way from Denali National Park to the town of Talkeetna. There, a group of visitors is planning to fly onto a glacier. They then want to ski down the glacier. But the weather has other plans…

The group really wants to get to the glacier to ski. "So, can we go today?" one of them asks. But the answer is not a good one. "Uh, not until the **pilots**[1] are comfortable with the weather," replies their **guide**[2] Colby Coombs. He then explains that the clouds are too low, so the group cannot fly. It's too unsafe.

Colby Coombs and Caitlin Palmer are both experienced mountain guides. They run a climbing school. They teach beginner climbers and help experienced climbers to reach the top of Denali. Denali is a mountain that is also known as Mount McKinley. It's the highest mountain in North America.

---

[1]**pilot:** a person who operates an aeroplane
[2]**guide:** a person whose job is showing places to visitors

Colby and Caitlin are both very good climbers. They're not usually doubtful when they're in the mountains. But even they won't take a small plane out in bad weather. "It's kind of **ornery**[3] weather," says, Colby. "You usually have to **factor in**[4] a day or two to **put up with**[5] bad weather."

So, Colby and Caitlin decide on another plan. Instead of taking the group to ski down a glacier, they will take them to climb up one. They plan to take the group to a glacier that they can drive to in the car: the Matanuska glacier.

---

[3] **ornery:** bad
[4] **factor in:** include
[5] **put up with:** take into consideration; allow for

Infer Meaning

Read the second paragraph on page 8 again. Analyse the phrase below. To what does each underlined word refer?

'they will take them to climb up one'

Matanuska is a very big glacier—it's 27 miles long and two miles wide. The name 'Matanuska' comes from an old Russian word for the **Athabascan Indians**[6] who live in the arca. The glacier is in a low area that has many trees around it. It formed 2,000 years ago, but it's always moving and changing. It's also always difficult to climb.

---

[6] **Athabascan Indians:** [æθəbǽskən ɪndiənz] a group of native people who live in Alaska

The group gets ready to climb one of the Matanuska glacier's formations—a 30-foot wall of ice. At the base of the wall, Caitlin explains how to climb it, and it's not going to be easy. "The most **stable**[7] you're going to be is when you have all the points of your **crampons**[8] sticking on the ice," says Caitlin.

Caitlin then suggests ways to use crampons. They can help people climb up ice securely and safely. "Front points in...**heels**[9] down," she says. "And if you're going to place a tool," she adds, "[place it] really solid[ly]."

---

[7] **stable:** strong; secure
[8] **crampon:** a type of climbing tool for ice or snow that fits on the shoe
[9] **heel:** the rounded back part of the foot

tool

wall of ice

heels

front points

crampon

The hike across Matanuska is beautiful, but it can also be very dangerous. One summer, a young man fell into an opening in the ice called a **cirque**,[10] and died.

There are also stories of beginner hikers who get lost and almost die from the cold. In addition, there are **crevasses**[11] everywhere. The climbers have to be careful; they could easily fall in. If they fall into a crevasse, it will be very difficult to get out. Perhaps it will be impossible.

---

[10] **cirque:** [sɜːrk] a round opening in the ice
[11] **crevasse:** a long deep opening in the thick ice of a glacier

The group walks slowly and carefully across the glacier. It's very cold; they have to keep moving to stay warm. Finally, they reach solid ice. They're at **the heart of**[12] the glacier at last.

At this point, the climbers have a wonderful view. They can see a glacial lake with many **seracs**[13] in the background. Seracs are large pieces of blue glacial ice that stick up in the air. The glacier creates these seracs as it slowly moves.

Colby explains that an area with many seracs is called an 'ice fall.' He also adds that the seracs can make the area unsafe. This is because they are very big and may fall. He says that a good climber would not hike below an ice fall. It's just not safe.

---

[12]**the heart of:** the centre of
[13]**serac:** [sɪræk] a large piece of glacial ice

crevasse

The group enjoys climbing the glacier. It's hard work, but Colby and Caitlin make it look easy. It's a very special feeling when the members of the group reach the top of another ice wall. "OK, I made it!" says one of the beginner climbers happily.

Alaska is home to a large number of glaciers, about 100,000 in total. The people in this group can now say that they have successfully climbed one of them—Matanuska. Now, they only have 99,999 more glaciers to climb!

What do you think?

1. Would you like to climb a glacier?

2. Why or why not?

3. Imagine you are going to climb a glacier.
   What three things will you take with you?

After You Read

1. In Alaska there is usually:
   A. rain
   B. snow
   C. fog
   D. all of the above

2. On page 4, the word 'it' in paragraph one refers to:
   A. the village of Talkeetna
   B. the weather
   C. Alaska
   D. Denali National Park

3. What is another name for Denali?
   A. Mount McKinley
   B. Athabasca
   C. Alaska
   D. Talkeetna

4. The group decides to drive to another glacier because the weather is too dangerous to fly.
   A. True
   B. False

5. Which of the following is a good heading for page 11?
   A. Large Glaciers
   B. Low Area Without Trees
   C. All about Matanuska
   D. A 2,000 Year Old Tree

6. Which of the following is true about Matanuska?
   A. There are only a few trees in the low area.
   B. The glacier's name comes from an old Russian word.
   C. The glacier is 3 miles wide and 27 miles long.
   D. The glacier never changes.

7. On page 12, what does the word 'explains' mean?
   A. decides to do something
   B. believes in something
   C. thinks about something
   D. gives information about

8. Which of the following is safe on a glacier?
   A. a crevasse
   B. a cirque
   C. a crampon
   D. a serac

9. What does Colby think about an area with a lot of seracs?
   A. A good climber will not hike there.
   B. A good climber can hike there.
   C. A good climber will stop and rest there.
   D. A good climber should climb there.

10. On page 18, the word 'special' can be replaced by:
   A. common
   B. wonderful
   C. worrying
   D. interesting

11. In this story, people _____ across and _____ up a glacier.
   A. drive, fly
   B. fly, ski
   C. hike, climb
   D. ski, drive

ICE CLIMBING FOR BEGINNERS

Ice climbing is similar to mountain climbing. However, instead of being on hard stone, ice climbers move up, down, and even across walls of cold, glassy ice. There are two types of ice climbing. The first type involves climbing over ice and hard snow on the side of a mountain or glacier. The second type involves climbing up water that has become ice—for example a frozen waterfall. Climbers say that both can be difficult and that both require very serious attention.

A Frozen Waterfall

ice axe

boots

rope

Ice climbers need good boots, strong ropes, and an ice axe.

One difficult thing about ice climbing is that the ice in one place can change from day to day. It can, even change from hour to hour. The best way to go up a wall of ice in the morning may not be the best way to come down again later. Ice climbers have to learn how to see differences in the ice. They must also be able to change their plans accordingly.

Three things are very important to help keep ice climbers safe when they climb. First of all, they need special boots to keep their feet warm. These boots also help to stop them from falling when they put their feet down on the ice. Secondly, ice climbers need an ice axe. They can use this axe to make small openings in the ice. They can then carefully place their feet in the openings. The third important thing they need is a rope system. Climbers often only use one rope, but sometimes they use two.

Now let's take a look at something special that all ice climbers put on their boots—crampons. Crampons hold climbers' feet securely as they place them on the ice. The crampons actually go into the ice and give the climber a secure place to step. People say that crampons are responsible for saving many climbers' lives because they stop them from falling.

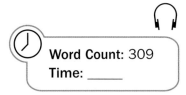

Word Count: 309
Time: _____

Vocabulary List

cirque (15)
climb (2, 7, 8, 9, 11, 15, 16, 18)
crampon (12)
crevasse (15)
factor in (8)
fine (3, 4)
fog (3, 4)
glacier (2, 4, 7, 8, 11, 12, 15, 16, 18)
heel (12)
hike (2, 15, 16)
ice (3, 12, 13, 15, 16)
mile (3, 11)
national park (2, 4)
ornery (8)
pilot (7)
put up with (8)
rain (3, 4)
serac (16, 18)
ski (2, 4, 8)
snow (3, 4, 12)
stable (12)
sunshine (3, 4)
the heart of (16)
wind (3, 4)

HEINLE
CENGAGE Learning

Footprint Reading Library: Alaskan Ice Climbing
Series Editor: Rob Waring

Director of Content Development: *Anita Raducanu*
Director of Product Marketing: *Amy Mabley*
Director of Global Marketing: *Ian Martin*
Marketing Manager, EMEA: *Stefanie Walters*
Assistant Marketing Manager: *Stephanie Blanchard*
Editorial Manager: *Bryan Fletcher*
Associate Development Editors: *Victoria Forrester, Catherine McCue*
Editorial Assistant: *Jason Seigel*
Content Project Manager: *Dawn Marie Elwell*
Senior Print Buyer: *Mary Beth Hennebury*
Contributing Editor: *Sue Leather*
Contributing Writers: *Colleen Sheils, John Chapman*
Editorial Project Manager: *Rebecca Klevberg*
Production Project Manager: *Chrystie Hopkins*
Production and Design Services: *Studio Montage*

Cover Photos:
(t) © Melissa McManus/Getty Images, (c) © Eastcott Momatiuk/Getty Images, (b) © Joel Sartore/National Geographic Image Collection.

Photography Credits:
TP © Joel Sartore/National Geographic Image Collection, 4-5 © Danita Delimont /Alamy, 6-7 © Medford Taylor/National Geographic Image Collection, 8 © MIMOTITO/Getty Images, 9 © WorldFoto/Alamy, 10-11 © Panoramic Images/ National Geographic Image Collection, 11 © Chad Case/Alamy, 14-15 © Alaska Stock LLC/Alamy, 18-19 © Paul A. Souders/CORBIS, 22 © James Balog/Getty Images, 22-23 © PhotoDisc/ CD-Elements, 23 © blickwinkel/Alamy.

Illustration Credits:
2 (t) © Mapping Specialists, Ltd. Madison, WI, USA, 2-3, 12-13, 16-17 © Jim Effler for American Artists Rep., Inc.,

Library of Congress Control Number: 2006908272
ISBN 13: 978-1-4240-1051-6
ISBN 10: 1-4240-1051-9

Heinle
High Holborn House
50-51 Bedford Row
London WC1R 4LR
UK

Cengage Learning is a leading provider of customized learning solutions with office locations around the globe, including Singapore, the United Kingdom, Australia, Mexico, Brazil, and Japan. Locate our local office at:
international.cengage.com/region

Cengage Learning products are represented in Canada by Nelson Education, Ltd.

Visit Heinle online at **elt.heinle.com**
Visit our corporate website at **www.cengage.com**

Printed in China.

2 3 4 5 6 7 8 9 10 — 11 10 09 08

PRE-INTERMEDIATE
800 HEADWORDS
A2

EXCITING ACTIVITIES

Alaskan Ice Climbing

Many people visit Alaska to see the beautiful national parks. One group of visitors wants to fly into a national park and go skiing. However, the weather is really bad. Will the visitors be able to get to the park? What will they do there?

Welcome the sights and sounds of the world with the *Footprint Reading Library*. Accompanied by original video material developed by *National Geographic Digital Media*, this is the first non-fiction reading series to present fascinating real-world stories in three formats: print, audio, and video.

Heinle, a part of Cengage Learning, is a leading provider of materials for English language teaching and learning throughout the world.

Visit elt.heinle.com

ISBN-13: 978-1-4240-1051-6
ISBN-10: 1-4240-1051-9

90000

9 781424 010516

NATIONAL GEOGRAPHIC

The Story of
THE HULA

Footprint Reading Library with video from National Geographic

To the Student,

The *Footprint Reading Library* introduces you to sights and sounds from around the world! With original video material developed by *National Geographic Digital Media*, these readers offer exciting real-life stories in print, audio, and video. We invite you to enjoy the stories and to develop your English language skills in three easy steps:

Read the stories and learn new vocabulary.

Listen to the stories on audio.

Watch the stories come alive on video.